THE EVERYDAY ADVENTURES OF
PAPA & PAI
HOLE IN THE FENCE

WORDS & PICTURES
BY PAPA PAWS

*For our little burrito Harley,
furever in our hearts.*

*For our sweet snuggle bug Macy,
always first to alert us of danger.*

Sign up for our email newsletter at www.papaandpaws.com
for cute and fuzzy updates and get a free short story eBook!

ISBN 978-1-956850-01-7

Library of Congress Control Number:
2021920082

First edition published January, 2022

A HAPPYLAND PRESS BOOK

That's a LOT of *holes* in our yard!

They are all *different* sizes too.

Small
holes.

Medium
holes.

LARGE
holes.

Doggie Door for Fence

What We Need

- Measuring Tape
- Pencil
- Calculator
- Saw
- Hammer & Nails
- Paint
- Paintbrush
- *Help from Doggies!*

Door Flap Lifts Up

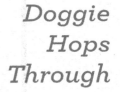

Doggie Hops Through

THANKS FOR READING!

Papa publishes our books independently
and he really appreciates your support.

LOOKING FOR MORE ADVENTURES?

VISIT WWW.PAPAANDPAWS.COM
to see all the books in
The Everyday Adventures of Papa & Paws
children's book series.

CPSIA information can be obtained
at www.ICGtesting.com
Printed in the USA
LVHW072001211221
706850LV00019B/458